Journaling For Discovery and Delight

Creative Prompts for Your Journey

Dawn Paoletta

ISBN - 10:1975898621
ISBN-13: 978-1975898625

Dedicated to:

Jesus my gracious Redeemer,

my best friend & hubby, Angelo
and
my beautiful daughter, Katherine.

CONTENTS

Dawn Paoletta

.

Remember, the blank page is an invitation to discover and delight in who you are now, who you have been, and who you are becoming.

Enthusiastically, Dawn

ACKNOWLEDGMENTS

I want to acknowledge and thank my original RJD ladies: Susie Klein, Pam Steiner, Cecelia Lester, Carolyn Wiley, Kathryn Ross. I also wish to extend gratitude to these women who have offered up their talents, gifts and support to me in a multitude of ways: Lauree Andrews (my BFF), Kel Rohlf, Lynn Morrissey, Dawn Maurice, Stacy Artis and Pamela Manners (my BBFF). Additional thanks for the freely offered edits and encouragement by my Thursday Writers leader and friend, Linda Langlois. Additionally, I want to thank those who have followed my blog and waited patiently for me to make good on publishing. You all have contributed to this journey and offering. I pray it blesses you back as you have blessed me.

It's the deep breath before the plunge.

~ J.R.R. Tolkien

BENEATH THE SURFACE AND BEYOND

I have been sharing my journal-keeping journey online since I began my first blog, *Beneath the Surface: Breath of Faith*, in 2011. During that time, I connected with fellow bloggers who also shared a love for journaling. With their support and encouragement, I hosted an online journal gathering, monthly, called *Random Journal Day*. We would dig into our archived writings hidden in closet journal piles and glean words we'd written longhand in the past. We would choose something from one of those formerly forgotten journal entries and write up a blog post featuring some or all of the handwritten remembrances. These intimate, memorable, sometimes profound, musings led us to surprising new insights and drew us close together into a small community of fellow writers.

Perhaps it was our distance that allowed us to grow closer, to not stumble on distractions that otherwise may have hindered our ability to connect. Each of us lived hundreds if not thousands of miles apart. But here we were, sharing our personal writings, thoughts, memories, pains, struggles, and joys despite the distance. The community remained small by today's standards, but what it lacked in size, it made up for in character and graciousness, offering the feel of a tight- knit community to visitors and kindred alike.

I truly am indebted to this small group of women who gave me a safe nest to grow in my early blogging days and the gentle nudges, encouragement, and support to test my wings and fly.

Since childhood, writing has been a therapeutic outlet for me. Early in my journal-writing journey, I felt that it was only about writing the good stuff. That belief could not be further from the truth. My greatest writing and most profitable moments in journal keeping have come through writing the *hard* stuff. The stuff we really would rather not have as part of our story. But there you have it...if we wait to start journaling when life gives a picture-perfect day, or if we are only willing to write during those days, we will never reap the most beautiful benefits of journal keeping. I long to share this gift with you as we journey together.

The statement below is true, and I encourage you to test its validity for yourself:

Be brave in your journal. Write from the most naked part of your soul. It will set you more free than you've ever been before.

A few things to know for your journaling journey

1. Daily Journaling. Each prompt is an opportunity for you to explore in your journal. With each daily invitation to write, there is at least one alternative prompt to help inspire your pen one way or the other! The important thing is to be inspired.

2. Using the Prompts. I drafted these prompts in my journal during a brainstorming session in January of 2014. After participating in a couple of online art/journal challenges, which I enjoyed, I felt that I would like to host my own. The prompts themselves vary greatly, from silly and fun to deep and reflective. There is no right or wrong way to tackle the prompts; simply let them lead. You might feel led to write a poem or a short paragraph. You might feel led to sketch, doodle, collage, or springboard off in an unanticipated direction with your pen. YAY! That's all excellent. *Inspiration happens when we stop worrying about*

getting it right or fitting in the box but instead explore wherever it leads.

3. What You'll Need. A journal and pen. Period. However, you are free to use whatever you'd like. You can used lined sheets or blank, an altered book, or scrapbook. Whatever works for you. A few of the prompts offer an alternative creative prompt for those who'd like to play, but a pen and journal is all you absolutely need.

4. Using the Schedule, but... Originally the prompts followed a 21 day schedule. The idea that if you write for 21 days - it's slightly less intimidating than 30 or 31 days but still will help create the momentum needed for supporting your journaling habit. Feel free to create your own boundaries and perimeters if you write regularly. For instance, You could make your 21 days specifically for supporting a fixed routine. Use the a timer and stop writing after a set amount of time. Or you might write specific days of the week and follow the prompts in order. Another way to vary is by random selection. Whatever works!

JOURNAL KEEPING, WRITER'S BLOCK AND PERFECTIONISM

"Promise me you'll always remember: You're braver than you believe, and stronger than you seem, and smarter than you think." ~A.A. Milne

Meet my therapist and faithful friend: the Journal. As one who carries a journal mostly everywhere and always – saving me a small fortune in psychiatric fees, I assure you – I'm hoping to encourage you in your own journal-keeping journey, whoever you are and wherever you are headed. Whether you write for fun, work, or some other compelling reason, whether you are a creative person looking to overcome your fear of writing or a non-creative person trying to tap your creativity, the bottom line is this: You have a wellspring of inspiration within you, and I hope I can help you see that which is already there.

In these prompts, we will cover **three basic areas of focus** concerning the act of writing of every kind:

First, for me, writing anything usually begins in my journal, so I will share a few thoughts on *Journal Keeping* and the power and possibilities therein.

Second, I am no expert, but I know what it is like to have to write something and feel the weight of pressure that blocks the mind, creativity and flowing words. The writer's enemy across the board is *Writer's Block* . Perhaps we can explore how it might be accepted as a gift, and see how this shift changes our perception, and ability to set words free again.

Third, I believe the only thing potentially worse than dreaded Writer's Block and deadly to creativity of all kinds is *Perfectionism* .
I hope that my words today on these three topics will bring a fresh insight or two, or just a refreshing splash of inspiration to your writing life, wherever it is at this moment.

Journal Keeping

I usually start my day writing. Every day. I grab my coffee and current journal, and on most days, my Bible. During this time, I am certainly not regimented in my approach. I might read a few chapters in the Bible, or I might just sit, watching the birds, listening to the quiet as I rock gently, out back on the veranda. There are days when words come easy, pouring forth from my pen after reading passages, listening, praying. Other days, I barely scratch out a line. *But it is the showing up, day in and day out, that pays off.* There are days I need to ponder more deeply my words, revelations, thoughts. There are days I need to listen harder to that still-small voice within. Oh, and then there are days when busy-ness and life intrude. No worries, the Good Book and the Journal travel well. But if I have to pick one, I carry my journal. God's Word is engraved in my heart, but my journal must be with me wherever I am just in case I receive a word, need to vent (I go to the journal most times, not the phone or friends), or need to feel the connection between myself and my God.

The pen is my chariot, bringing me ever higher to the heavenlies. Even when it pours forth ugliness. The heart is more naked than we know. We all are ultimately laid bare. *It is a worthy goal to have no pretense in living or writing.*

The journal is the place from which everything else in my life (especially creatively) springboards. Prose for poetry, blog posts, and other writings are natural outflows of my journal writing time. I am not writing for an audience when I journal, but certainly that which starts privately on my pages prompts most of what you see published publicly. Sometimes I just scratch out a title, a thought, sentence, or paragraph randomly, while journaling, which gives rise to more. I scribble the idea as a seed on the page and return my mind to the prior writing entry before the little seed bursts forth further, interrupting my train of thought.

Is it my ADHD, or is it just the creative spark in action? Either way, journaling regularly, those seeds come.

Writer's Block
Deadlines and To Do lists. They either make you swoon with anticipation or slow your every ounce of creativity to a torturous drip, drip, drip. It's one thing to write when you are excited about the topic, but what about when you have to write for a deadline, money, or commitment? I can't speak to the writing for cash but for a scant job (or two) many years ago when I wrote a poem for a jewelry company about birthstones for a pittance. Of course, the dreaded endless papers written for college and presentations are another issue. The word deadline can be the kiss

of life or death for creativity, right? But here are my two cents...my pittance, if you will:

Because I write in my journal so frequently, my richest times of creative flow have already been poured out. *When I feel dry, I just look back and pull inspiration from my more fluid days of writing.* Guess what that does? It *surprises* me and *releases* me from the clamp of Writer's Block, because I can see I had a plethora (love that word!) of ideas and ramblings just waiting from a while back.

Perspective is important for the days when you feel the impending deadline coming and find yourself staring at the computer screen or blank page as a deer staring into the headlights. You know what's coming, but you just can't move. Well, get out of the road and read your old stuff.

For a real shocker, read some of your college papers. Or old journals, secret hidden writings, blog posts etc. *Read your own writing. It will do more for you than reading anyone else's.* Before you conclude that I am an eccentric egomaniac, I hope to assure you that I am. No, just kidding. I read myself, because I am real in my journals and I need to remember who I am, warts and all, when I am in the desert with my writing or afraid I can't make or live up to the deadline! I also see how my writing has changed and grown. I like to edit my older writings. I catch things that I missed on previous edits and, simultaneously, I am reminded that I am not a totally sucky writer. Hooray! The same is true for you. So, the next time you feel ready to choke your computer, will you try this and let me know how it goes?

Perfectionism
So you treated yourself to that pretty, brand new journal. But now, when you look at the pages, you want to try to, ya know, be perfect. *Sigh*. Listen to me. Forget this "being perfect" crap. Go look in the mirror. Go! Now! Get a wooden spoon from the kitchen drawer, and hit yourself. Now, repeat to your reflection: *"My messy is just fine, I don't need to be perfect, or write perfectly, I just need to keep it real and the rest will flow."* Now see that fresh new journal page. See all the empty pages before you? I want you to grab a cup of coffee, take a big, sloppy sip, and let it trickle down the outside of the mug. DO NOT get a coaster or a napkin. Instead, set it in the corner of the first perfect page of your journal. Let it sit there for a minute. Now pick it up and have another sip and do whatever you want with the cup. See that stain? Good. Now you don't have to worry anymore about how everything needs to be so perfect in your journal, in writing, or in life. Life is messy. Let your writing reflect what is real. *Your message needs to be filtered by only one thing: your own authenticity.* I mean, your messy, coffee-stained, crooked life is the one that will

keep you connected to who you really are *beneath the surface.* Your voice comes through beautifully when it's a bit mussed up.
Let all you write, create, just reflect the real you. Obviously, your journal holds safely your musings before you polish and shine them up for the world to see. But the more you allow yourself your journal space to hash it all out, the more powerful your authentic voice becomes in public spaces.

SIMPLE STEPS FOR JOURNALING SUCCESS AND SATISFACTION

"Because God is a writer, it is only natural that we, created in His image, are writers also."
Lynn D. Morrissey

I often hear excuses when the conversation turns to writing or journal-keeping.

"I wish I had more time to write."

Or

"I've tried keeping a journal before but stopped."

Another common concern with journal-keeping is privacy. Revealing your heart's condition and committing it to paper can be a scary proposition. The possibility that someone else might see something that you did not want to share can hinder the beautiful freedom that journal-keeping can offer "But, what do I write about?" is yet another potential stumbling block for journal keepers.

Whether you have never kept a journal before or are an on again/off again journaler, I want to offer a few tips to help you find the time to squeeze journaling in and to keep journaling on. I also want to urge you to find the journal-keeping endeavor that suits this season of your life and allows the habit to continue for the long term so that the benefits and blessings will be experienced in time, thus reaffirming the commitment to write for the simple, personal joy experienced by *you*, the journal keeper.

There are a number of different ways to keep your journal, and the journal itself is a highly adaptable tool to utilize in your *journal-keeping journey* (go ahead and say that three times fast).

Consider the season of your life. When my daughter was small, my journal entries often drifted off (literally!) mid-sentence. I would plop down exhausted after a day of chasing down my tiny tot, only to discover that sleep was all that I could muster. I would find pen markings in my sheets from falling asleep with an open pen! During that season of inconsistent writing, I would faithfully put my journal in the bottom of the stroller and head out for an afternoon walk. If I was lucky, and she had enough activity earlier, she would drift off into a sweet sleep and I would find my way to a park bench, journal and Bible by my side, for a few quiet moments. I felt that God multiplied the time and blessed me with insights that I enjoy looking back on even now.

Carry your Journal wherever you go. I am not sure when it was that I started to do this, but I continue to do this most always. I am rarely without my journal. One never knows when an idea, inspirational thought, poem, or revelation might come. If you carry a small journal in your purse when that moment comes, you will be ready to scribble it down.

KISS it (Keep It Simple, Sweetie). The best way to start a new habit or get back on track with a habit you want to keep up is to keep it simple. There are a few ways you can make it happen. First, identify how and why you want to journal. Are you wanting to take word pictures to look back on in the days ahead, maybe reflect about the inner workings of your heart? Or, maybe you want to count your blessings or gifts, Ann Voskamp style. Keeping it simple will be different for different people. Consider the following possibilities for writing in your journal: one day a week, just 5 minutes a day, 15-30 minutes every other day, before bed, writing just 5 gifts, a few blessings or thanksgivings before you shut off the light, daily morning paragraph prayer, an evening summary of the day, or even collecting one quote a day that is meaningful to you each day. Phew! That's a lot of keeping it simple options. A *small daily commitment* to your journal will keep the words flowing and will feel less intimidating when faced with the blank page.

Keep it private, but accept the possibility of exposure. You could go to extreme measures to secure the privacy of your journal. But it is better to make peace with the possibility of being exposed. Either keep your journal in an off-limits place, or begin to embrace the reality – as I have – that ultimately, there is nothing that will not be revealed in eternity. I do understand that, as we share, we need to have some level of trust that we are able to safely lay our hearts on the table, or paper as the case may be. In my home, it is an understanding that journals are private. However, I do keep many of them in a closet out of sight, trusting that my privacy will be respected.

Whatever! Whatever? Yes, whatever. Remember, you do not have to be a great writer to benefit from journaling. As a matter of fact, you don't have to be a "writer" at all. Forget about good grammar, throw the idea of performance out the back door... just shut the front door! (Could not resist that one.)

Put away your phone and don't worry about impressing anyone.

Give yourself permission to write *whatever* you want.

It's okay to sit with the intimidation a bit, too. Remember, if you still can't find it in you to write on that wide open page, grab your coffee, take a slurpy sip making sure the coffee (or tea!) drips down the side and put that cup on that journal page. Pick it up, do it again...now splash some on...there, now you are an Artist! Take a breath, and after that dries, sit down and observe. Write the first word that pops into your head. Blank mind? Look around, what do you see? TV guide? Magazine? Books? Write what is in front of you that grabs you...Now there, you broke the ice. Relax. Listen to your breath. Tune into your own heartbeat. If you are feeling brave, go ahead and write your thoughts. It's not about getting the words right, it is about getting the pen flowing long enough that your courage grows. It's about coaxing the soul out from hiding. Most days, our souls are hiding, bullied by busy-ness and superficial living. Journaling can get you to that place of peace, empowerment, grace, and truth.

5 Minute Writing Challenge!

Here's a page dedicated to reflecting and writing about your experience with this book Jot a few notes, favorite prompts or tips you want to incorporate into your journaling practice regularly.

_____

_____

_____

_____

_____

_____

_____

_____

_____

_____

_____

_____

_____

_____

_____

_____

_____

_____

_____

_____

_____

_____

_____

THE 21 PROMPTS CHECK LIST

- ○ **1– Love is in the Air**
- ○ **2 – Exploring the Ordinary**
- ○ **3 – Furry Friends**
- ○ **4 – I Fancy a Fairy Tale**
- ○ **5 – Lists, Lists, Lists**
- ○ **6 – Rewriting Scripture**
- ○ **7 – Feast or Food Show**
- ○ **8 – Everybody Wants To Rule The World**
- ○ **9 – Art Pass**
- ○ **10 – One Day Visit**
- ○ **11 – Rich and Famous**
- ○ **12 – Literary Love**
- ○ **13 – 24 Hours With God in History**
- ○ **14 – Your Perfect Day**
- ○ **15 – The Letter**
- ○ **16 – Every Picture Tells A Story**
- ○ **17 – Second Chances**
- ○ **18 – A Providential Moment**
- ○ **19 – The Power of Words**
- ○ **20 – When I Was a Little Girl…**
- ○ **21 – Oh, The Places We'll Go!**

Track your Journaling journey by checking or shading the circles upon completion.

1 – Love is in the Air

"A lady's imagination is very rapid; it jumps from admiration to love, from love to matrimony in a moment." Jane Austen

Welcome to Prompt 1 of 21 Days of Journaling. Take a breath, read the prompt below, and see what moves you or what motivates your pen to move. Grab your journal and a choice beverage, find a favorite place to write, and make yourself comfortable to just be still and enjoy wherever your mind goes.

Prompt 1: Write about how you met your significant other. Don't get stuck in making it a perfect recollection; recall what is precious, amusing, and unique! Have fun remembering.

Alternatively:

1. Write a short story or vignette in which your main character meets their significant other. Enjoy letting your imagination dream up the characters, the setting, and every creative detail as you wish!

2. Write a letter to your future (or current) spouse. What do you want to tell them about yourself, your hopes and dreams for the future, life and family, or the journey thus far.

3. Write about your first crush/first love.
Have fun, and choose the main prompt or
alternative based on your mood today! There are
no rules, whatever strikes your fancy...just open
your journal and write.

P.S. Yes, you can tweak the prompts. As a fellow
journal writer just said to me *very* once (ahem,
Lynn M.), "There is no wrong way to journal!"

2 – Exploring the Ordinary

"The 'show business,' which is so incorporated into our view of Christian work today, has caused us to drift far from Our Lord's conception of discipleship. It is instilled in us to think that we have to do exceptional things for God; we have not. We have to be exceptional in ordinary things, to be holy in mean streets, among mean people, surrounded by sordid sinners. That is not learned in five minutes."
~ Oswald Chambers

Life is not lived in climactic moments but in the slow dripping of a faucet, the tick-tocking of the clock, the hum of cars passing by and crickets chirping throughout the night. Our lives are a quilt of woven-together scraps from time, events, celebrations – but we hang onto the simplest memories from childhood and beyond. Learning to appreciate the day-to-day ordinariness of life is a sign of maturity. Perhaps, in the ordinary, there is something magical to be discovered after all. Join me as we explore the ordinary.

Prompt 2: Complete the sentence, or springboard as you feel led into a journey into an ordinary moment in time. *It was an ordinary morning.. .*

Alternatively:

1. Ponder where this Dickens opening leads you: *"It was the best of times, it was the worst of times, it was the age of wisdom, it was the age of foolishness, it was the epoch of belief, it was the epoch of incredulity, it was the season of Light, it was the season of Darkness, it was the spring of hope, it was the winter of despair, we had everything before us, we had nothing before us, we were all going direct to Heaven, we were all going direct the other way..."*

2. Write about what comes to you as you reflect on the following quote: *"Life isn't a matter of milestones but of moments."* Rose F. Kennedy Don't be afraid to just ponder. **Pondering is like marinating for writers and journalers** . No need to rush; sit with your wild mind for a bit. You might be surprised where it leads. As you feel ready, open your journal and write! Don't force it. Tenderly invite whatever comes. Enjoy the journey.

3 – Furry Friends
"You know what I like most about people? Pets."
Jarod Kintz

*"Until one has loved an animal, a part of one's soul
remains unawakened." Anatole France*

Furry Friends. I've had a few, how about you? Our
family currently includes one dog, one
bunny, and two cats, in no particular order. OK, the
cats insist they are first. Today's prompt may
have you feeling nostalgic, or teary eyed, or both.

Prompt 3: The pet I'll never forget...
Although we love all the pets that come into our
lives, focus on writing about the one that comes
to your mind first.

Alternatively:

1. Write about the pets you've had over the years
and their significance in your life.
2. Random pet memories. Allow your mind to
remember the sweetest, silliest, most memorable
moments, characteristics, and experiences you've
shared with fur friends.
3. Choose one of your fur friends and make a
special memory acrostic poem or list with their
name.

Take the prompt as it leads. Trust, and enjoy the
process.

4 – I Fancy a Fairy Tale

"Every man's life is a fairy tale written by God's fingers." Hans Christian Andersen

What is your favorite fairy tale? Do you have one? If you've ever dreamed of toads turning to princes or enjoyed a tale of imaginative proportions, you will enjoy today's prompt. Don't be intimidated, but today we have a Fairy Tale Challenge! First, let's look at the definition, and then we can see where it leads.

fairy tale:
noun
1. a story, usually for children, about elves, hobgoblins, dragons, fairies, or other magical creatures.
2. an incredible or misleading statement, account, or belief: *His story of being a millionaire is just a fairy tale.*

Prompt 4: Write your own Fairy Tale. You're the star, or give yourself a bit part. Share a message or lesson you've learned about life, love, or even fairytale expectations. Go wherever the prompt takes you. Don't worry about doing it right. Give yourself fairy wings and fly with it!

Alternatively:

1. Doodle in your journal a magical creature of your choice.

2. Collage images and words that evoke a fairytale feeling.

3. Write about your favorite fairy tale and share why it has meaning for you.

4. Write about one of the many writers of fairy tales, and explore what inspires you in their writing style.

5. Any combination of the above as you feel inspired!

5 – <u>Lists, Lists, Lists</u>

"The list is the origin of culture. It's part of the history of art and literature. What does culture want? To make infinity comprehensible. It also wants to create order." ~Umberto Eco

Whether you think of a to-do list or bucket list, whatever you prefer for this exercise, we are a people of many lists. We make lists for the grocery store and for our days. Some of us love them and live by them, others abhor them, and I bet most of us use them in one capacity or another.

Prompt 5: Today's Prompt is to go at it and make a list of things you'd like to try, do, or learn. List as many things you can think of, even if the possibility of achieving it seems unlikely. Make it like a bucket list on steroids. Write every single thing that pops into your head, and don't discriminate. Just list those ideas as they come.

Feel free to respond with images from magazines or sketches if you feel inspired to do so. Or add them after you have made your list.

Alternatively:

Read the quote below and journal your own thoughtful response to Mr. Eco's assertion:

"We have a limit, a very discouraging, humiliating limit: death. That's why we like all the things that we assume have no limits and, therefore, no end. It's a way of escaping thoughts about death. We like lists because we don't want to die."

~Umberto Eco

6 – <u>Rewriting Scripture</u>

One of the most powerful things I have done is to rewrite God's word into prayers in my journal. I often will write different versions of the same verse as it speaks to me in time. But just as we are taught in school to articulate in our own words something we have read or learned, it can be helpful to apply this to our Scripture reading. It can be an exhilarating and exciting endeavor to rewrite scripture as we reflect on it prayerfully. The Word of God is living, active, and powerful (Hebrews 4:12). God is able to speak to us through His Word.

I'm not saying we should twist the meaning into something it isn't, but instead just allow it to lead us deeper. So often, we rush through familiar passages. We don't savor and allow the words to linger on our palate. But as we taste, we will surely find the Lord's goodness.

Prompt 6: Rewrite The Lord's Prayer or Psalm 23 in a way that makes it personal and powerful to you. Enter into Scripture and see where it leads as you do this exercise. Linger over each verse and ask God to speak to your heart.

Alternatively:

1. Take any passage or chapter of Scripture that you feel you want to meditate on, read it, reflect on it, and rewrite it in your own words.

2. Rewrite a passage, verse, or verses into a prayer, poem or song. I experimented with a combination of prayer and poetry using Isaiah 40:28-31 - as shown here with my words italicized.

Lord, you promised...
I hold You to your Word,
though I tremble and doubt
before all I have seen and heard.
Your Holy Spirit sings songs to my soul...

Do you not know?
Have you not heard?
The Lord is the everlasting God,
the Creator of the ends of the earth.

Lord,
as quickly as the sun does rise,
I see my child growing up before
my eyes...

He will not grow tired or weary,
and his understanding no one can fathom.

7 – <u>Feast or Food Show</u>

What comes to your mind when I say "feast"? Is it famine? Thanksgiving, with its lush spread? Do you imagine castles, kings, and queens? Do you immediately imagine lavishly overflowing tables full of food, as in the Harry Potter scenes where the students gather to eat anything but cafeteria food, thanks to Dumbledore's magic. Whatever comes to your mind here is fine.

Prompt 7: Create an imaginary feast or remember a shared feast among friends. A feast can commemorate an event or person, can be an abundant and rich meal, and can have entertainment with many guests, or can simply be set before one or for two. You get to choose all the food and courses to be served at a sumptuous feast. You choose the decor, the entertainment, every last detail! Describe it all, invite whomever you'd like – and since this is imaginary, don't hold back! It can be as simple or decadent as you'd like. It can be spiritual or hedonistic. Let your writing lead you, and enjoy the journey!

Alternatively:

1. You have just been given your own cooking/food show. Your budget is unlimited. (Ha!) You can choose the kitchen decor for the show, you can choose and describe the focus and theme, you can be as creative as your heart desires. Are you a Giada, *Barefoot Contessa,* or Buddy Valastro? Do

you host a *Diners, Drive-Ins and Dives* or *Semi-Homemade* style of show? Do you favor Alton Brown or Paula Deen? If you enjoy cooking shows, you can have fun exploring your faves or create your own unique style and perspective! Take it wherever it leads. Don't be afraid to use dialogue in your writing to help see your persona.

2. Springboard off any of the following quotes:

"Marriage is a feast where the grace is sometimes better than the dinner." Charles Caleb Colton

"It always depresses me when people moan about how commercial Christmas is. I love everything about it. The tradition of having this great big feast, slap bang in the middle of winter, is an essential thing to look forward to at the end of the year." Richard E. Grant

"If you are lucky enough to have lived in Paris as a young man, then wherever you go for the rest of your life it stays with you, for Paris is a moveable feast." Ernest Hemingway.

MMM...I'm getting hungry already! What's cooking? Or rather, what's marinating in your mind? Write away, Journal Keepers!

5 Minute Writing Challenge!

Here's a page dedicated to reflecting and writing about your experience with this book and the first seven prompts. Jot a few notes, favorite prompts or tips you want to incorporate into your journaling practice regularly.

_____

_____

_____

_____

_____

_____

_____

_____

_____

_____

_____

_____

_____

_____

_____

_____

_____

_____

_____

_____

_____

_____

8 – <u>Everybody Wants To Rule The World</u>

I am probably aging myself by asking this question, but here goes...do any of you remember the song *Everybody Wants To Rule The World*?

Your writing prompt today may take you places you never imagined you would go. Or perhaps you have imagined it, as a child. Well, the fact is that, in our flesh, we all want to rule the world. Or at least our own little world, yes? It is the nature of the beast, our human default. I want control, you want control, and BAM – that's the way the world goes round. Sorta...

Today, you get to have a pass. Like passing *Go* on the Monopoly Board. You get to rule the world. No, you can't exactly be God; Eve already tried that, and we know where that story goes. However, for your writing journey today, collect your 200 dollars and circle the board as you like. You have a *get-out-of-jail-free* card, and the sky is the limit.

Prompt 8: If I were ruler of the free world...

Alternatively:

1. If I were queen for a day...

2. If I had superpowers, they would be...

3. Princess or Villainess?

I feel a bit... Muahahahaha. How about you? Now, write, write, write! GO! Take the prompts wherever they lead, just be back by dawn! (Snort!)

9 – **Art Pass**

I remember watching the glee in my daughter's eyes as she painted and scribbled her way through her childhood years. I have so many pictures of her painting, and I saved way too many of her early scribbles, paintings, drawings, and artistic creations. Art gives us permission to be children again, free from the limitations of adulthood for a bit of time. Free to be, create, and dabble in making something from nothing. What could be more exhilarating?

This one is for your artistic side...hmmm...let's think this through. It is ok if you start in your journal, but take it outside of your journal if inspired!

Prompt 9: Take a Bible Verse and paint, sketch, collage, stamp, or otherwise create or re-create it.

All that being said and shared: DO YOUR OWN THING! Use whatever you have on hand, including colored pencils, markers, pastels, crayons. Or, just keep it black and white. Just have fun – I dare you!

Alternatively:

Write about a favorite artist or piece of art that is meaningful to you. Take the prompt any direction you want.

So many options, so little time...but *enjoyment is mandatory.*

Prompt 10 – <u>One Day Visit</u>

"What they do in heaven we are ignorant of; what they do not do we are told expressly." ~ Jonathan Swift

The doctrine of the Kingdom of Heaven, which was the main teaching of Jesus, is certainly one of the most revolutionary doctrines that ever stirred and changed human thought. ~H. G. Wells

He whose head is in heaven need not fear to put his feet into the grave. ~Matthew Henry

I am not getting any younger. You know how I know, aside of the obvious? Because a number of those I care about have left this present life. It's a strange thing as I ponder my youth and recalling the first time someone significant to me personally died. It rocked my world. I was about 19. I had little to no experience dealing with the reality of death and the afterlife. I knew about Heaven, but not much. I knew about Jesus, but not much more than 2nd Grade Catholic School.

Now, with my *50th birthday* on the horizon, I have said goodbye to many more than one loved one. There is a longing in us for those we love, and it never dies. It burns within us.

It's never easy to say goodbye, even if we believe it is temporary. Sometimes there are things left unsaid. We know there are no tears beyond His glorious gates, but in the meantime, we wait. We long to be reunited with old friends, acquaintances, loved ones. Today our prompt may be challenging or joyous, or maybe both. Be gentle with yourself. Be brave. Either way, take the prompt as you wish.

Here it is:

Prompt 10: You have a One Day Pass to visit heaven and spend the day with a loved one who has gone on ahead. What will you want to say or do?

Alternatively:

Make a list of those who have passed, or choose just one person to focus on that has had some influence, impact, or significance in your life. Write out a brief prayer to God for each one, thanking Him for their contribution to your life and His amazing grace and infinite knowledge. Praise God with your pen for His unfathomable and faithful ways, and for Jesus, the One who makes Heaven possible for all who believe.

So don't be afraid; you are worth more than many sparrows.

"Whoever acknowledges me before others, I will also acknowledge before my Father in heaven. But whoever disowns me before others, I will disown before my Father in heaven. (Matthew 10:31-33)

11 – <u>Rich and Famous</u>

I recently wrote a local author and nationally syndicated columnist with regard to a moving piece he had written. In the e-mail I sent, I shared a blog post that I had written in response to the same topic, which I felt was rather inadequate when compared with his well-articulated work. I was delightfully tickled when he responded, as I honestly had no idea if he would a) actually read the e-mail, b) respond to e-mails in general, or c) bother reading the post I shared.

To my surprise, he did a, b, and c. He also gave me his thoughts on my writing AND then ended his e-mail with these words: *"Don't forget me when you're rich and famous!"*

His e-mail response was short, gracious, and a pleasant surprise. Even more surprising was when my writing instructor informed me that she regularly writes him and gets no response.

So, I wonder...what will I do when I am rich and famous? HA!

Prompt 11: Your prompt (as if you don't know), is to finish the sentence, "*When I'm rich and famous...*" or "*When I'm rich and famous, the first thing I will do...*" Continue in any direction with this prompt. Just have fun with it.

Alternatively:

1. You are disgustingly rich. Describe in detail a few of your favorite indulgences. You can be humorous, ridiculous, and ludicrous. What does a day in the life look like for you?

2. You are suddenly wealthy and able to do whatever you wish for yourself and others. What do you do? What don't you do? What might you do that you have not done before? Be imaginative. Discover yourself in new ways. Be radical. Or absolutely predictable. Walk through it with words...

3. You are suddenly thrust into fame. Describe how, why, and what it is like. What was it that made you famous? How will you use the attention? Imagine what it would be like, what might change?

Feel free to write this as fiction if you feel inspired. As always, respond to the prompts anyway you want.

12 – <u>Literary Love</u>

Chances are, if you are on this writing journey, you not only love to write, but you also love to read. Today's prompt is all about the books you love, or have loved, to read. Originally, I wrote the prompt to focus on a favorite devotional, but as I considered this further, I realized that the power of a great book to speak to us is not limited to Christian literature alone. The power of great literature or a timely *read* can speak volumes to us personally, and sometimes great insight and inspiration can come from unexpected places. For instance, years ago I read *The Witching Hour* by Anne Rice. I was heading off to Washington, D.C., for a Personal Training Conference and wanted a book for the trip. I picked it up on a whim, but it remains one of the most amazing surprises I have ever read. The imagery of New Orléans painted in Rice's amazingly vivid writing etched its way into my mind forever. I have been to New Orléans thanks to the detailed descriptions of her writing!

I love books, and my love is not limited to one genre. I especially love classic children's books, as well as memoirs and biographies. My favorite childhood book was *The Lion, The Witch and The Wardrobe* by C.S. Lewis. On the other hand, my mom gave me *The Hobbit* to read at the age of 12, and I just could not get into it. I have since tried again, and although I love the *Lord of The Rings* movies, I have not been able to get through Tolkien's tales yet! I can never get through Chapter One. *Sigh.*

So, today we delve into our love for great reading of all kinds. From Oswald Chambers to Stephen King. Hans Christian Andersen to Suzanne Collins. From classic literature to current creative writing. From *Harry Potter* to *Jesus Calling*. Let's have fun considering the *reads* that have stayed with us, the stories that speak to us, the words that minister most to us, and WHY. Think about what draws you in, fascinates you, challenges you and causes you to say "YES, I love this book (or author)!"

Prompt 2: Recall (one at a time for focused pondering and writing) your favorite book or story. Describe and explain what it is you love about this book or story. Include personal insights and take time to reflect on what makes this work especially significant or powerful to you.

Alternatively:

1. Explore the background and biographical information of one of your favorite authors. Note the details in your journal and make it be like a mini report or essay for yourself. Are there similarities in your tastes, style of writing, genre, history? Doodle it or Mind Map the details if you wish.

2. Write about your favorite devotional, inspirational, or spiritual book. Why is it your favorite? What does the author do that is unique? How does it draw you closer to God, or stronger in your convictions?

3. Same as above with your favorite devotional, inspirational or spiritual author. Look at their background and contrast the reality of their real lives with their writing. Record what you discover. *Have fun, discover your author influence, be inspired by your biggest inspirations!*

13 – 24 Hours with God in History

Imagine you could choose one time in history to spend with God for one day (24 hours). It's kind of like God, your Father, taking you, His kid, to work for the day. Where would you be in the continuum of time? What would you see and do? Are you with Him for creation? Walking with Him and Adam in the Garden? Are you in the desert with Him and the Israelites? Or in the chariot carrying Elijah? Do you hover with Him over the manger, or weep with Him at Gethsemane? What would you ask Him? What do you notice? What do you see?

Grab your Bible for this one. Choose the time in History you would like to be with God. Ask Him to show you something you have not seen before, as you seek His perspective and heart.

Prompt 13: Write about how you would spend 24 hours with God in history.

Alternatively:

Write a poem or prayer seeking God's perspective over a time or circumstance, concept, or idea in history that you struggle to understand, i.e. the Holocaust, Hiroshima, creation, world hunger. Anything that is a topic of burden, or a sticking point for you in your faith perspective. Using Scripture and prayer, ask for God's leading, share your struggle, and see where it leads. Be ready to listen.

Be still and quiet, then wait for His answers. Go where the prompt, His Word, and His prompting leads!

14 – <u>Your Perfect Day</u>

"Come away by yourselves to a desolate place and rest a while." Jesus

Because I often tend to cram too much into a day, this exercise helps me sit back, breathe and consider how to reorder my days to fit in things I might be skimping on or what I need to cut back on. I have taken this prompt a number of ways in my writing before, and I have used this as an exercise as a planning tool when coaching others. You can write a really imaginative piece with it and see where it leads, exploring how your ideal day would go. Or, you could allow the prompt to assist you as a tool to help brainstorm possibilities of having a better day with your specific goals in mind. Today, we imagine our perfect day and plan away with our pen...

When I did the *31 Days of Fitting in Fitness* on my former blog <u>Beneath the Surface: Breath of Faith</u>, I posed these questions for those on the journey. So, here they are for you and your life now...

Prompt 14: What areas of your life need to be kicked up a notch? What parts of yourself feel neglected: Physical, Intellectual, Spiritual, Relational? What small step can you take to nurture and nourish these aspects better, daily? What kinds of things make you feel refreshed, renewed, inspired?

Alternatively:

1. Let's consider whether our "perfect day" offers us the rest we long for but seldom experience? What might we do to experience the rest that allows us the flexibility and grace to adapt to the less-than-perfect days that make up the majority of our lives- knowing and trusting God loves us as we are, right where we are?

2. Another favorite author of mine is an example of one who knows the rest women long for, in Christ, throughout life. Elisabeth Elliot. Springboard off any of these quotes of hers:

"By trying to grab fulfillment everywhere, we find it nowhere."

"The life of faith is lived one day at a time, and it has to be lived – not always looked forward to as though the 'real' living were around the next corner. It is today for which we are responsible. God still owns tomorrow."

"If my life is surrendered to God, all is well. Let me not grab it back, as though it were in peril in His hand but would be safer in mine!"

"The heart which has no agenda but God's is the heart at leisure from itself. Its emptiness is filled with the Love of God. Its solitude can be turned into prayer."

Oh, and if your perfect day includes a hammock, there is no judgment here! Have fun! Happy Journaling!

5 Minute Writing Challenge!

Here's a page dedicated to reflecting and writing about your experience with this book and the second set of seven prompts. Jot a few notes. What changes are you noticing in your journaling/writing practice? What would you like to continue?

_____
_____
_____
_____
_____
_____
_____
_____
_____
_____
_____
_____
_____
_____
_____
_____
_____
_____
_____
_____

15 – <u>The Letter</u>

"A letter is a blessing, a great and all-too-rare privilege that can turn a private moment into an exalted experience." Alexandra Stoddard

"It does me good to write a letter which is not a response to a demand, a gratuitous letter, so to speak, which has accumulated in me like the waters of a reservoir." Henry Miller

"Letters are among the most significant memorial a person can leave behind them." Johann Wolfgang von Goethe

Prompt 15: Write a letter to a person who has impacted your spiritual life in either a positive way or a negative way.

The positive is usually easily written, but it may be hard to choose one person. Choose one person to start, but who knows, perhaps this will prompt you to recall and write (and even send) many letters to those who have blessed your walk with God.

The negative letter may be more challenging, but it may offer surprising insights and value, therapeutically, as you allow the words to spill out on paper.

See where the prompt leads you, and remember that God is faithful and can use writing as a vehicle to speak to you...let it be your burning bush!

Alternatively:

You can write a letter to anyone who has mentored or impacted your life in another realm, such as motherhood, career, sports...

Remember to write in your journal before God and yourself only. You can copy and edit the letter for sending if and when you decide, but remember your journal and all that is in it, is for your eyes only. (And God's, naturally!)

May He reveal great truths to you as you write and bare your soul!

16 – Every Picture Tells A Story

They say a picture is worth a thousand words. That's a pretty lofty load of words for one picture don't you think? But I will say that an image, painting, or drawing can certainly stir our thoughts and emotions, even arousing our physical senses. Perhaps there is some truth in the statement. Let's explore this idea, shall we? Have you ever had a photo or piece of art inspire your words? Have you ever used and image to spark your creativity while creating, writing a story or poem?

Once, as I sat checking out my Facebook feeds, a friend shared a picture of her daughter and the family dog, silhouetted in the morning light, on the bed. The image so grabbed me that it inspired me to write a poem based on my own canine relationship and personal feelings for our dog called "I Am Your Girl." A serendipitous creative moment.

Once, for April Fools on my blog, I used an image of a robbery as a writing prompt, and I made up a story that made it sound like I was present at the robbery. What a response I got! The combination of image and words was a hit.

Prompt 16: Your prompt will be a picture from magazine, old photo or printed from online. Cut

the image, glue it in your journal. Write whatever comes to you…

Alternatively:

Perhaps you'd like to draw today, so just pencil sketch something in your immediate eye view. If you are feeling inspired, sketch whatever sparks you. While visiting Maine, I spontaneously sketched the view of the mountains and lake outside our cabin, through the window, from my favorite seat in the living room, in my journal. PHEW. Have at it! And don't worry if you do not consider yourself an "artist." Everyone under the age of 8 understands you don't need to be an artist to draw! Be 5, 6, or 7 again. Drawing is required!

17 – <u>Second Chances</u>

Life is a continual journey of second chances, isn't it? The sun rises, mercies are new, and we awake to a new day of opportunity, a fresh start at the doorstep. Today, I offer you a couple of Coffee Shop prompts. Have at them as you will. As always, go wherever the muse takes you, and feel free to tweak that prompt to suit you and your muse!

Prompt 18: If you could, which moment from your life would you choose to re-live? Or, if you had a chance to change professions which new profession would you choose?

A few quotes for you to springboard off, if you'd rather:

"Because this is what I believe – that second chances are stronger than secrets. You can let secrets go. But a second chance? You don't let that pass you by." Daisy Whitney

"But it takes so little to help people, and people really do help each other, even people with very little themselves. And it's not just about second chances. Most people deserve an endless number of chances." Will Schwalbe

"[When it comes to God] We can't run out of second chances…only time." Robin Jones Gunn

"Gaining hope, I remember and wait for this thought:

How enduring is God's loyal love;
the Eternal has inexhaustible compassion.
Here they are, every morning, new!
Your faithfulness, God, is as broad as the day."

Lamentations 3:21-23 The Voice

18 – <u>A Providential Moment</u>

Today, your prompt is easy. I want you to write about a moment in your life, and I know there have been many, when you experienced God's providential intervention or care in a powerful way. Below are the Google search definitions. (Sometimes, I think Google is God's providential care for my blogging life!)

Prompt 18: Ponder the definitions below, then write about a moment in time that pops into your head when I mention *God's providential care in your life.*

Remember, this is your journal, and you can go as deep as you want with the prompt. Keep your writing private if you need to; share it only as God leads and you desire. Write for yourself and God first! Let this be your love language, an intimate connection between the One who knows you better than you know yourself. He will reveal Himself, but also show you what you need to know about *yourself* as well.

prov·i·den·tial
1. occurring at a favorable time; opportune.
"Thanks to that providential snowstorm, the attack had been repulsed."
2. involving divine foresight or intervention.
"God's providential care for each of us."

prov·i·dence

ˈprävədəns,-ˌdens/

noun

noun: **providence**

1. the protective care of God or of nature as a spiritual power.

"They found their trust in divine providence to be a source of comfort."

2. God or nature as providing protective or spiritual care.

"I live out my life as Providence decrees."

3. timely preparation for future eventualities.

"It was considered a duty to encourage providence."

Origin

late Middle English: from Old French, from Latin *providentia*, from *providere* 'foresee, attend to' (see provide).

19 – <u>The Power of Words</u>

"In the beginning was the Word, and the Word was with God, and the Word was God. He was with God in the beginning." John 1:1-2

"Writing and reading decrease our sense of isolation. They deepen and widen and expand our sense of life: they feed the soul. When writers make us shake our heads with the exactness of their prose and their truths, and even make us laugh about ourselves or life, our buoyancy is restored. We are given a shot at dancing with, or at least clapping along with, the absurdity of life, instead of being squashed by it over and over again. It's like singing on a boat during a terrible storm at sea. You can't stop the raging storm, but singing can change the hearts and spirits of the people who are together on that ship." Anne Lamott

Words. We love them, we hate them. We live by them. The fact is, they are powerful. The Bible says they are living and active. Maybe it's one of the reasons Jesus said that even the words we think are dangerous – because words we think become words we say, and even unspoken words hold power over us. It's why we are instructed to be careful what we ponder, and also to be careful what we allow ourselves to say. Ecclesiastes says, "Let your words be few…" And we are told we will give an account for every word we speak. Yikes. As we ponder the power of words, let's look at some of our favorite quotes, scripture and passages of writing.

Prompt 19: Take a Favorite Bible verse or quote and write about the importance of it on your thinking, your philosophy of life, your outlook, etc.

Alternatively:

1. Choose a specific theme or topic and use your journal to record quotes and/or scripture that are meaningful to you. If you're feeling creative, use your colored pens, or decorate as seems good to you.

2. Make a list of your top ten (twenty, thirty, etc.) favorite quotes. Or, you could just pick a theme and seek quotes to do with that subject. I do this with Google fairly frequently!

3. Open your dictionary randomly and discover some new words (maybe). Write using 10-20 of the words you find on the first two pages you open to.

Word Lovers: write away!

20 – <u>When I Was a Child…</u>

Today, we take a walk down memory lane. Some of us have had happy childhoods, others traumatic. I know that, for me, despite the difficulties, God's hand was evident. Yet there are times He shows me there is still growth needed, thinking that needs correcting, healing that can go deeper. The wonderful thing about our minds and God's grace is that we can train ourselves to seek out and focus on the good, not the bad. It is hard at first, but just as the light of early dawn grows brighter as the day goes on, the good looms larger and the bad is left behind in the darkness of yesterday's memory until it fades away completely into the past.

Prompt 20: In your journal, before God alone, start out with this line…

When I was a little girl…

Or, sorry guys- I'm not forgetting you, just need to step outside myself a bit. Forgive me, will you?
When I was a little boy…

Ponder the opening line. See where it leads you. Stay with it. Write what comes.

Alternatively:

1. Rewrite your childhood. Write in everything you needed but didn't get at this time. After you do this, offer up a prayer to God asking Him to reveal how His glory is manifested in your life despite the painful reality, or even maybe because of the

reality. Ask Him to minister to you and allow Him full access into any unhealed hurts, or long-term scars. Thank Him for His all-sufficient grace.

2. Revisit your childhood but focus on one specific memory that pops in your head. Stay with it, and write every detail you remember; write out every description and detail you can recall. Try not to judge the memory, yourself, or any of it – just stay with the details and scribble them out. Observe it all as a silent, neutral witness. After you record all the details, see what is prompted. Reflect and write your thoughts.

21 – <u>Oh, The Places We'll Go!</u>

Prompt 21: Your mission, if you choose to accept it, is to venture somewhere to write with your journal...outside of the ordinary routine of things.

The local library, coffee shop, park bench, museum, hotel lobby. I have journaled in DC on a tour bus at midnight, in an RV (as a passenger), on a train en route to Baltimore, beach-side in the Bahamas, and in too many coffee shops to calculate! Outside, inside, lakeside. Wherever you go, your journal can go.

Alternatively:

1. If you'd rather, try this: Take a few sheets of fun stationary or funky paper and go to your destination. Write about where you chose to go and why, then reflect and write whatever comes to you as you sit.

2. Go find or buy some stationery at a local stationary store, card shop, or gift shop – you can even pick out a card just for you. You have permission to go look at cards and find one that you absolutely love! Make sure it has lots of blank space, and even preferably a blank on the inside card. Now, grab a coffee, tea, or beverage of choice and write a note on the inside telling yourself why you chose the card you did. Adhere whatever you chose into the journal in a way that it is accessible

so it does not get lost. If you get a card, make sure to get the envelope to glue in your journal so that you can slide the card in and out to read when you wish.

A journal is a soul's best friend, and can be a direct connection from the writer's heart to the heart of God.

5 Minute Writing Challenge!

Here's a page dedicated to reflecting and writing about your experience with this book and make it your personal journaling companion. Concluding thoughts, favorite quotes:

_____

_____

_____

_____

_____

_____

_____

_____

_____

_____

_____

_____

_____

_____

_____

_____

_____

_____

_____

_____

_____

_____

_____

Congratulations!

If you have come this far and completed these 21 journaling prompts for the first time-Congratulations!

Take a moment and do a happy dance right now. You are one step closer to a lifetime of journal keeping. I hope you made a few discoveries along the way. My heart's desire is for you to delight in the act of journaling as it brings you closer to understanding yourself, others and the One who knows us and understands us better than we will ever comprehend .

Thank you for joining me on the journey!

RECOMMENDED RESOURCES:

Books:

At a Journal Workshop by Ira Progoff

Journal to the Self by Kathleen Adams

One to One: Self-Understanding Through Journal Writing by Christina Baldwin

The New Diary by Tristine Rainier

Love Letters to God by Lynn D. Morrissey

Writing To God 40 Days of Praying With My Pen by Rachel Hackenberg

Poem Crazy Freeing Your Life with Words by Susan Goldsmith Woolridge

Fragrant Fields Poetic Reflections for Journaling by Kathryn Ross

Writing Past Dark Envy, Fear, Distractions and Other Dilemmas in the Writer's Life by Bonnie Friedman

The Hidden Writer Diaries and The Creative Life Alexander Johnson

Helpful Links:

*The Progoff Intensive Journal Program for Self-Development : Intense and powerful. CEC provider for Nurses, Social Workers, Ministry Personnel. **http://intensivejournal.org/index.php**

*Home page of Dr. James W. Pennebaker (Psychologist/Professor) **http://homepage.psy.utexas.edu/homepage/Faculty/Pennebaker/Home2000/JWPhome.htm** Click on *Writing and Health* for practical advice on journal writing through trauma and emotional upheaval for increased mental and physical health.

*The Center for Journal Therapy : http://journaltherapy.com/ Kay Adams offers excellent resources for journal keeping. Click for Journal Writing : A Short Course

*Bullet Journal website http://bulletjournal.com/ Ryder Carrol's method for organizing, planning, tracking etc.

If this journaling book has been useful to you I would love to know. I would also greatly appreciate your review if you feel inclined to write one and would love to see your images on Social Media too!Tag me!
#TheJournalEnthusiast

@enthusiastdawn on Twitter

enthusiasticallydawn on Instagram

Dawn Paoletta on You Tube

Let's keep in touch!

Join me for a variety of Journaling Journey Posts and more at Enthusiastically, Dawn!

Stay tuned for my next books!

Dawn Paoletta is a life enthusiast who loves to juggle words, chug coffee, chat about faith, and journal excessively. She enjoys hanging out with her hubby, daughter and family pets in Narragansett, RI and shares her passion, poetry and prose at her blog, Enthusiastically, Dawn.

Journaling Workshop Notes

<u>Journaling Workshop Notes</u>

Journaling Workshop Notes

Journaling Workshop Notes

Journaling Workshop Notes